Light in the Dark

Written & illustrated
by Stacey McNeill

ISBN: 978-1-7396782-3-4

I CAN NAVIGATE THE STORMS, AND I KNOW CALMER SEAS ARE COMING

I CREATE MY
OWN LIGHT

I TRUST IN
THE TIMING
OF LIFE

I GIVE MYSELF
TIME TO BE STILL

I HAVE
EMPATHY

IT'S OK TO
CHANGE MY MIND;
~ IT'S A
SIGN OF
GROWTH

I AM WORTHY OF RECEIVING LOVE

I AM
PROUD OF HOW FAR
I HAVE COME

I AM ON MY OWN
UNIQUE JOURNEY;

I ACCEPT I MAY FEEL LOST
SOMETIMES, BUT I KNOW I
WILL ALWAYS FIND MY WAY

I ASK FOR AND ACCEPT HELP -
I DON'T HAVE TO DO IT ALL MYSELF

I AM NOT ALONE

I INVITE
HAPPINESS
AND
ABUNDANCE
INTO MY LIFE

I DESERVE TIME TO REST

I ACCEPT THINGS THAT HAVE HAPPENED IN THE PAST; I LEARN FROM THEM, AND I CAN MOVE FORWARD

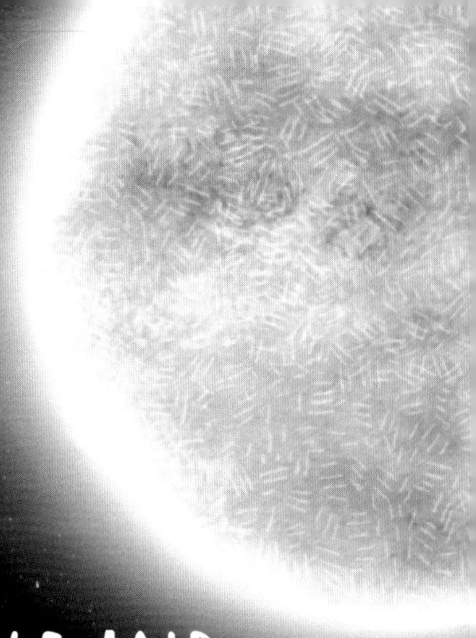

I AM WHOLE AND COMPLETE ON MY OWN- OTHERS ONLY SUPPORT ME

I AM PRESENT

I WELCOME
THE WISDOM THAT
COMES WITH
EXPERIENCE

I AM
ENOUGH

I HAVE
COMPASSION

I KNOW
THINGS WILL
BE OK
EVENTUALLY

I LIVE MINDFULLY
AND IN THE PRESENT

AMAZING
THINGS ARE
COMING MY WAY

I AM GROWING AT
MY OWN PACE

I CAN
CHOOSE
WHO I LOVE

I GIVE MYSELF KINDNESS

I OPEN MY HEART TO NEW THINGS

IT'S OK
TO LET GO

I AM GRATEFUL FOR
ALL I HAVE

I HAVE HOPE
IN TIMES OF
GRIEF AND PAIN

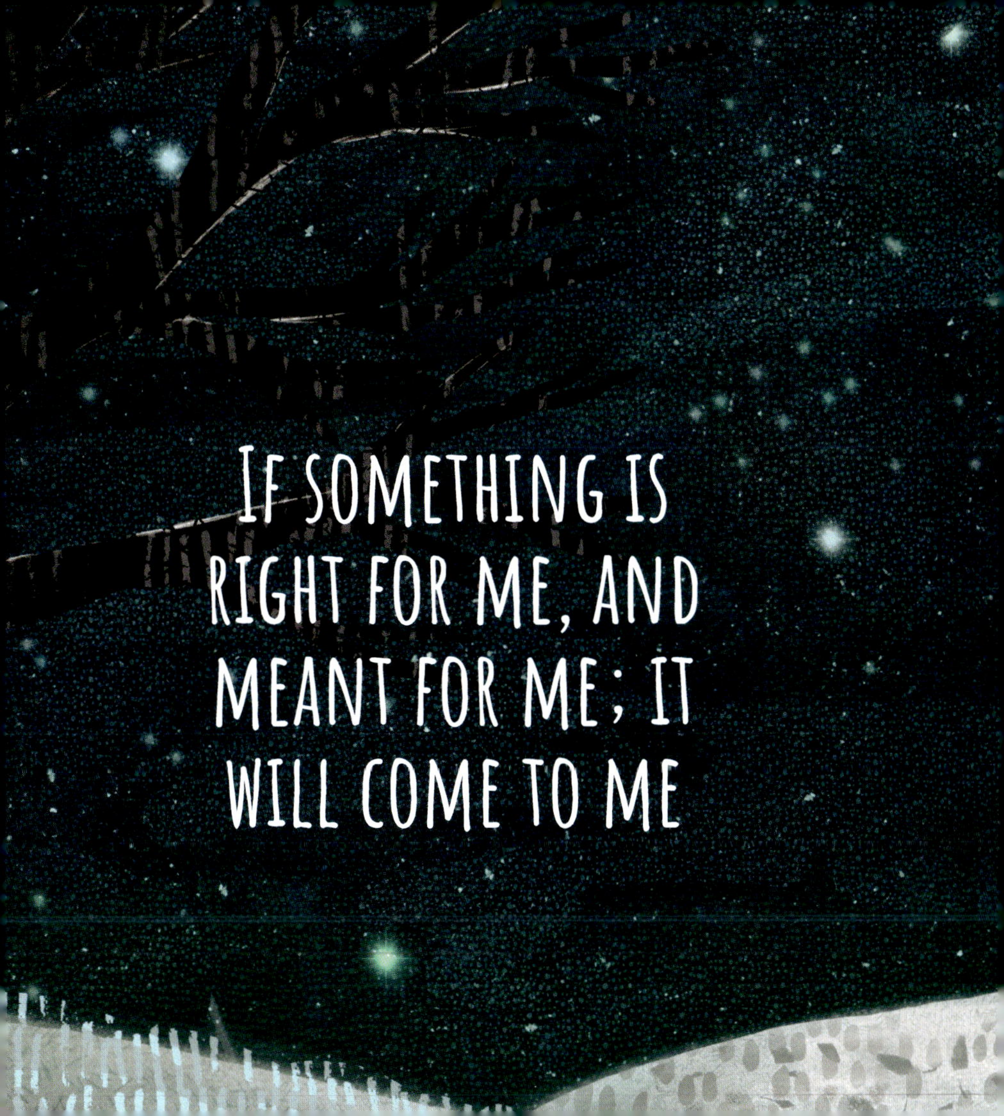
If something is
right for me, and
meant for me; it
will come to me

I BELIEVE
IN
MYSELF

MY SENSITIVITY IS A BEAUTIFUL STRENGTH

I CAN BE WHO I WANT
TO BE
WITHOUT JUDGEMENT

I AM OPEN TO RECEIVE WHAT IS MEANT FOR ME

I MAKE
A DIFFERENCE

I CREATE
SPACE FOR
OPPORTUNITY

I AM LOVED

MY THOUGHTS AND FEELINGS ARE VALID AND IMPORTANT

I TRUST
AND FOLLOW
MY
INTUITION

I AM ON
MY OWN PATH

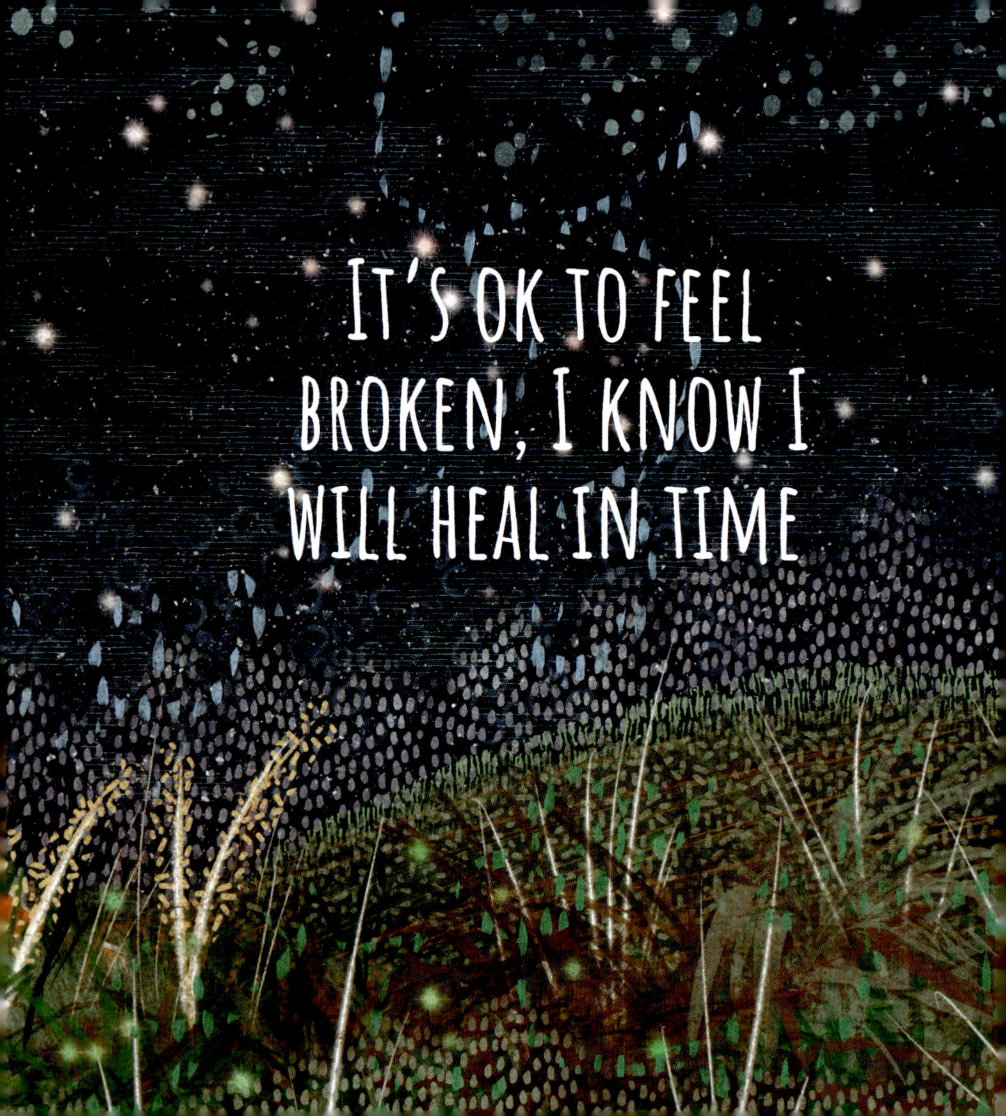

It's ok to feel broken, I know I will heal in time

I AM CAPABLE AND RESILIENT

EVERY
SITUATION IS
TEMPORARY

I AM ABLE TO KEEP GOING

I AM
A GOOD FRIEND

I AM ABLE TO
FORGIVE

I SHOW KINDNESS

IN ALL I DO

I ALWAYS HAVE
IT IN ME TO SHINE

I OPEN MY HEART
TO
RECEIVE LOVE

MIRACLES DO
HAPPEN

SAYING 'NO' IS
OK SOMETIMES

I KNOW

MY OWN
HEART
AND MIND

I HAVE THE POWER TO MAKE
MY DREAMS A REALITY

It may be slow,
but I am healing

Hello! I'm Stacey – author, illustrator and creator of 'Fox Under The Moon'

My 'Fox Under The Moon' artwork series is for all ages – it is inspired by the simplicity of everyday life, and the complicated emotions that go with it.

Through my words and illustrations you will meet an anxious, but inquisitive fox, and the wise old moon. The two become friends, and I hope that their warm and whimsical world can bring some encouragement and love to yours.

For books, prints, cards, gifts and wholesale enquiries, visit:

www.foxunderthemoon.co.uk